SADIE
AND THE
SADISTS

PAUL
MULDOON

SADIE
AND THE
SADISTS

◡◠ **EYEWEAR** PUBLISHING

SPECIAL EDITION
PAMPHLET

First published in 2017
by Eyewear Publishing Ltd
Suite 333, 19-21 Crawford Street
Marylebone, London W1H 1PJ
United Kingdom

Cover design and typeset by Edwin Smet
Cover photograph by Alija (Getty Images)
Author photograph by Oliver Morris
Printed in England by TJ International Ltd, Padstow, Cornwall

ISBN 978-1-911335-90-0

*Eyewear wishes to thank Jonathan Wonham for his
generous patronage of our press.*

WWW.EYEWEARPUBLISHING.COM

PAUL
MULDOON

is an Irish poet and professor of poetry,
as well as an editor, critic, and translator. Born in 1951 in
Portadown, Co. Armagh, Northern Ireland, he published his first
book, *New Weather*, in 1973, at the age of 21. From 1973 he worked as a pro-
ducer for the BBC in Belfast until, in the mid-1980s, he gave up his job to
become a freelance writer and moved to the United States. Muldoon is
the author of twelve major collections of poetry, including *One Thousand
Things Worth Knowing* (2015). He has also published smaller collections,
works of criticism, opera libretti, books for children, song lyrics and
radio and television drama. His poetry has been translated into twenty
languages. Muldoon served as Professor of Poetry at Oxford University
from 1999 to 2004 and as poetry editor of *The New Yorker* from 2007 to
2017. In addition to being much in demand as a reader and lecturer, he
occasionally appears with a spoken word music group, Rogue Oliphant.
Paul Muldoon is a Fellow of the Royal Society of Literature, the Amer-
ican Academy of Arts and Sciences and the American Academy of Arts
and Letters. In addition to the Pulitzer Prize, he has received an Amer-
ican Academy of Arts and Letters award in literature, the 1994 TS Eliot
Prize and the 2006 European Prize for Poetry. He has been described by
The Times Literary Supplement as "the most significant English-language
poet born since the second World War." Roger Rosenblatt, writing in
The New York Times Book Review, described Paul Muldoon as "one of the
great poets of the past hundred years, who can be everything in
his poems – word-playful, lyrical, hilarious, melancholy.
And angry. Only Yeats before him could write
with such measured fury."

SADIE AND THE SADISTS

I'M NOT ONE

So many bands achieve renown
Getting their look down
As they roll into town
For a charity gig

So many of our country folk
Think it's a joke
To take a poke
At the sacred black pig

So many things
Will wear a nose ring
To show off what they've done
But I'm not one

So many who've been up in arms
May find themselves charmed
By your smarm
And sweet talk

So many modern troubadours
Add strings to the scores
So their songs will soar
With the hawk

So many things
Will extend a wing
To the 12 gauge shotgun
But I'm not one

[instrumental]

So many seem to catalogue
Living high on the hog
While dog eats dog
Along with the mush

So many look beyond the mud
To find fresh blood
At the first bud
Of a hydrangea bush

So many things
Will come back in the spring
They'll come back with the sun
But I'm not one

RAIN OR SHINE

[instrumental]

Our hearts were light
Our wedding night
Though our vows were solemn
For thirty years
We've kept well clear
Of the gossip columns
In sickness and health
Our healthy disregard
For sickness and health
Still holding hard
Back in Syracuse
Where we first took aim
Kahn and Le Corbusier
Were in the frame
All our efforts to blend
Ones we now transcend
The groundplans we draw
Down to the deadline

The end we'll see through
Rain or shine

A sole sunbeam
Can bring a gleam
To the hill's raw umber
Though at Belmont
They just don't want
To play by the numbers
Our opening act
Won't act their age
Our opening act
Have set the stage
And in Buffalo
Through a thunderstorm
The Rolling Stones
Stay true to form
They know in their guts
Nothing's open-and-shut
But Mick and Keith
Won't wither on the vine
They'll strut their stuff
Rain or shine

It looks like even Moses
Left under a cloud
It looks like even Joshua
Liked to play pretty loud

[instrumental]

It's not the earth
But a narrow berth
That the meek inherit
That we might get
A little wet
Won't dampen our spirits
Till death do us part
It's party time
Till death do us part
We're in our prime
For in Saratoga
We've come to terms
With the going being soft
While we stand firm
That we're made of clay

Will carry the day
We may fall from grace
But not off cloud nine
We'll stay the course
Rain or shine

SIDEMAN

I'll be the Road Runner
To your Wile E. Coyote
I'll take you in my stride
I'll be a Sancho Panza
To your Don Quixote
Your ever faithful guide
I'll stand by you in the lists
With our marketing strategists
I'll be your sideman, baby,
I'll be by your side
I'll be I'll be I'll be by your side

I'll be a Keith Richards
To your Mick Jagger
Before he let things slide
I'll be Sears to your Roebuck
Before he took the headstaggers
And opened nationwide
I'll support you at Wembley
I may require some assembly

But I'll be your sideman, baby,
I'll be by your side
I'll be I'll be I'll be by your side

I'll be McCartney to your Lennon
Lenin to your Marx
Jerry to your Ben &
Lewis to your Clark
Burke to your Hare
James Bond to your Q
Boo-Boo to your Yogi Bear
Tigger to your Pooh
Mary Godwin to your Shelley
Groucho to your shtick
Cyd Charisse to your Kelly
Beatrice to your Benedick
Trigger to your Roy Rogers
Roy to your Siegfried
Fagin to your Artful Dodger
I guess I'll let you take the lead

[guitar solo]

I'll be Chingachgook
To your Leatherstocking
A blaze of fur and hide
Our shares consolidated
Our directorates interlocking
I'll be along for the ride
I'll be at Ticonderoga
I'll be there for you at yoga
I'll be your sideman, baby,
I'll be by your side
I'll be I'll be I'll be by your side

REPEAT OFFENDER

It takes one card overspent
Or missing one month's rent
To put you on the street
One trip to Nepal
Was a clarion call
That I should beat a retreat
It takes one raincloud
To cast a shroud
Over the Fourth of July
One sidelong look
Was all it took
For you to catch my eye
Once is enough to have anything to do
With guys who pretend to be tender
But when it comes to loving you
I'm a repeat… I'm a repeat…
I'm a repeat offender

That one chord thrown down
At the top of 'Brown
Sugar' gets me on my feet
I raise one eyebrow
When I ponder how
To retweet my own tweets
It takes one shot
In a parking lot
To get hepatitis B
That one left hook
Was all it took
For Frazier to stop Ali
Once is more than enough to eat Irish stew
In South Bend after a bender
But when it comes to loving you
I'm a repeat... I'm a repeat...
I'm a repeat offender

[bridge]

Last night I saw your name on a marquee
On the outskirts of Lonely
I hate to think your appearance might be
One time only

[instrumental]

It takes one idea to float
A paper boat
Or the Seventh Fleet
One twit talking tosh
Can put the kibosh
On a royal meet and greet
It takes one near
Death experience to hear
A wee small voice
That one last book
Was all it took
To put me off James Joyce
My chances of returning to Kathmandu
Are slender… slender… slender
But when it comes to loving you
I'm a repeat… I'm a repeat…
I'm a repeat offender

FATTY LIVER BLUES

I'd given up the brandy
I'd given up the rum
Then I splashed out on nose candy
I paid a tidy sum
And so it wouldn't wither
Or lose its side effects
The coke would be delivered
The next day by FedEx
That night in Cincinnati
I did a line or two
I woke up with the shivers
Some oily residue
Now I've got them fatty liver
Got them fatty liver blues

I'd given up the vodka
And the eau de vie
That didn't stop the drug squad
Coming after me
My unshod pony slithered

As I rode through the snow
One arrow in my quiver
Two strings to my bow
I was eating bison patties
Washed down with Mountain Dew
On the Little Bighorn River
I partied with the Sioux
Now I've got them fatty liver
Got them fatty liver blues

[instrumental bridge]

I'd given up the whiskey
I'd given up the gin
But then Miss Zabriskie
Slipped me a Mickey Finn
She'd been all comehither
All lickety split
She'd offered me a sliver
Of ham with slivovitz
Jersey City is so ratty
Her hair was ratty too
Now it seems my caregiver

Cares for someone new
And I've got them fatty liver
Got them fatty liver blues

TILL I MET YOU

Till I met you
I was a flag without a pole
A scrawl without a scroll
A soloist without a cue
A gadfly-sting without a herd
A thing without a word
Till I met you

Till I met you
I was a bird without a perch
A larch without a lurch
A merchantman without a crew
A butterfly without a jar
A sky without a star
Till I met you

There was a sense of something unfulfilled
When I decided to leave
As if we both still
Desperately wanted to believe

Till I met you
I was a scar without a scab
A jape without a jab
A labyrinth without a clew
A bellyful without a bag
A bull without a rag
Till I met you

PUT ME DOWN

I want to be the transport ship
From which we both lift off
I want to be the cartridge clip
In your Kalashnikov
I want to play wargames in which
We get to use live rounds
For when you've left me
For dead in a ditch
At least you've put me down
Put me down put me down
At least you've put me down

I want to be the rifle butt
You hold close to your breast
I don't care if your comments cut
Right though my Kevlar vest
I want to be within your scope
Your thoughts are so profound
I guess I'm still hoping against hope
You won't just put it down

Put it down put it down
You won't just put it down

To my being on tenterhooks
Whenever you're around
I want to be the instruction book
You simply can't put down
Put down my love put down
The manual you can't put down

I want to be the haversack
That hangs around your neck
I'd follow you to hell and back
From this same helideck
I want to be the smoke that clears
Over the battleground
When the cry goes up for volunteers
I trust you'll put me down
Put me down put me down
I trust you'll put me down

HERE IN TINSELTOWN

Lynn hitchhiked from St Louis
With just her makeup pouch
Her eyes always looked dewy
From the casting couch
Lynn was one who entered
The city of gold
To find at its center
Only a centerfold
Though she still thanks the stars
For her starlet roles
Those years of tending bar
Have taken their toll
She used to look quite festive
Now she wears a frown
For it seems she might be resting
Here in Tinseltown
Yeah it seems Lynn might be resting
Here in Tinseltown

Lon rode in from Albuquerque
Already saddlesore
He went straight from beef jerky
To ragout of wild boar
Lon wore a white sombrero
In the Valley of the Kings
Yul Brynner was part pharaoh
Part Villa part Swamp Thing
Though it often seemed that Lon
Was cowed by Clint and Duke
It was rockets over Saigon
Had his Appaloosa spooked
He used to work in westerns
From sunup to sundown
But it seems he might be resting
Here in Tinseltown
Yeah it seems Lon might be resting
Here in Tinseltown

Some hang up their spurs
To be chefs or chauffeurs
And some are lost to herb
They'll all do lunch

With that studio bunch
Who use 'partner' as a verb
When I say 'partner' it's a noun
Here in Tinseltown

Len schlepped from the Saint Lawrence
Via the isles of Greece
With an Argonaut's abhorrence
Of the golden fleece
But when he came to edit
New footage with the old
Len had to take some credit
When the credits rolled
Though he kneels before the golden calf
At least it is in prayer
He can't say if it's wheat or chaff
But there's something in the air
He's so used to purple vestments
And blue surgical gowns
It seems he might be resting
Here in Tinseltown
Yeah it seems Len might be resting
Here in Tinseltown

GO-TO GUY

If you've spent the house-keeping
I'm guilty by default
If my wounds are weeping
They're crying out for salt
I'm your sugar daddy
When the Dow slumps
Your '89 Caddy
When you hit those 'speed bumps'
When you need another stock to buy
When you need another trade to ply
When you need another stitch to tie
I'm your go-to guy
Go-to guy go-to guy
I'm your go-to guy

If your horses are restive
It's because of my horseplay
If my mood is festive
It's because you carried the day
Last night in the E-Quad

With the mechanical mugwumps
At Starbucks or Pequod
Where you manned the pumps
When you need another sock in the eye
When you need another fish to fry
When you need a first mate to say aye
I'm your go-to guy

Aye-aye aye-aye aye-aye aye-aye
Aye-aye aye-aye aye-aye

Though I bring home the bacon
You're still high on the hog
If I feel forsaken
It's not that you've lain with a dog
I'm your Elizabeth Bowen
When the cat jumps
I'm your Leonard Cohen
When you're down in the dumps
When you need another lock to pry
When you need another kite to fly
When you need another hope to die
I'm your go-to guy

Go-to guy go-to guy
I'm your go-to guy

SADIE AND THE SADISTS

I joined Sadie and the Sadists
In late '76
My hairstyle was part mohawk
Part Elvis's cow's lick
It was so punk
To get blind drunk
On Guinness spiked with gin
Most dangerous were those
Who'd pierced their nose
With a safety pin
We came close to making it
With our first LP
Sadie and the Sadists
Were like family to me
Family... family...
Yea Sadie and the Sadists
Were like family to me

I joined Clive of India
In early '78

It seemed frock coats and ruffles
Were never out of date
The life of prog
Had me go the whole hog
On the back of Pink Floyd's pig
Our agent reckoned a song
At leat twenty minutes long
Could still be big
And we came close to making it
With our third LP
Clive of India
Were like family to me
Family… family…
Yea Clive of India
Were like family to me

[instrumental]

Pyscho Billy and the Orangemen
I joined in '81
The bass I played was upright
A double-barrelled shotgun
The bass drum to boot

Was built to suit

By Loudens of Lambeg

Things are never dull

When you have a skull

Tattooed on your middle leg

We came close to making it

With our fifth LP

Psycho Billy and the Orangemen

Were like family to me

Family… family…

Yea Psycho Billy and the Orangemen

Were like family to me

EVEN WITH YOU

It's true we would go forth
With our high school diplomas
From Dallas Fort Worth
To Shawnee Oklahoma
We rode two sorrel mares
We named the Constant Nags
The chestnut was a spare
It carried all our swag
We hit the Shawnee Mall
On North Kickapoo
Shopping could be such a ball
Even with you
Even with you
Even with you Ms Faithless
Even with you

It's true we would set sail
Across the South Pacific
To bag a sperm whale
A mystic hieroglyphic

The oyster house on Sansom
Had given us a whiff
Of what comes over the transom
Of a Carolina skiff
Harpoons are hard to shoot
From dugout canoes
But whaling could be such a hoot
Even with you
Even with you
Even with you Ms Faithless
Even with you

And everybody knew
You and I were overdue
For our big duet
Then it all fell through
The whale we found was blue
A blue whale set to get
Even with you
Get even with you

It's true we would light out
For Indian Territory

With a Pawnee scout
And his hard luck story
When the roof caved in
All our hopes were crushed
I've eaten from a tin
Since after the gold rush
Let's uncover the past
With our skeleton crew
Mining could be such a blast
Even with you
Even with you
Even with you Ms Faithless
Even with you

LOUD AND CLEAR

I hear the Beijing mission
Were probing much too deep
The dirt they're used to dishing
It's no longer dirt cheap
Your giving poverty a try
Has hit another snag
Since you stopped off in Shanghai
And bought three Kelly bags
And now you claim a Birkin's
Prohibitively dear
I hear you baby
I hear you loud and clear
As to who's behind the break-in
I hear you loud and clear

Now the Shanghai connection
Have clarified their role
They've scoured our visa section
Envisaging a mole
I hear the suit from Singapore

Was made by Edwin Wong
A bank account labelled 'offshore'
Was traced back to Hong Kong
When you say time in prison's
The least of your fears
I hear you baby
I hear you loud and clear
As a person of interest
I hear you loud and clear

I couldn't make out that stuff about your lover
And you going undercover
Like you'd gone under a cloud
But the dispute over two detachable collars
Costing an extra fifty dollars
Was heard loud and clear baby
Loud and very clear

The issues we once skirted
Have fallen round our heads
The media were alerted
Once you went off your meds
I hear your good name's still besmirched

From all the mud you fling
The fact you've left me in the lurch
Won't sit well with Beijing
Though since you've come much closer
To whisper in my ear
I hear you baby
I hear you loud and clear
If you're asking for some closure
I hear you loud and clear

BIG TWIST

It turns out Planet of the Apes
Is our own planet Earth
The priceless Maltese Falcon
Has virtually no worth
All those statues and statuettes
Have proved a total sham
Though Liberty had once seemed set
On winning the Grand Slam
Your falling for me that first day
Was the first clue I missed
And that you've loved me all along
Is clearly the big twist

It turns out that in Chinatown
Incest gives a fresh slant
To a retired blade runner's
Being a replicant
I'd guessed you must be cyber-born
Till you opened the dam
And wept to read a unicorn's

Last origami-gram
The thought I'm secretly your prey
Is not one I've dismissed
For that you've loved me all along
Is clearly the big twist

[instrumental bridge]

It turns out at the Bates Motel
Cross-dressing's the new fad
Princess Leia's Luke's sister
Darth Vader is their dad
A starfighter has the Blue Book
Value of your Trans-Am
The way you suck that bone you look
More and more like your mam
A galaxy far far away
May be shrouded in mist
But that you've loved me all along
Is clearly the big twist

ENOUGH OF ME

The monk despairs of his maker
Sheetrock the two-by-four
The beach renounces the breaker
Jersey the Jersey Shore
The biographer comes to hate
Her latest biographee
It's come to me of late
You've had enough
Had enough you've had enough of me

The team gives up on the teamsters
Cowboys mud in their eyes
The seam fights shy of the seamstress
Along the inner thigh
The foundation stone loves to diss
The capstone it aimed to be
As I've managed to miss
You've had enough
Had enough you've had enough of me

You've had enough of my seat-of-the-pants remarks
Enough of my speaking off-the-cuff
My holding forth so unbuttonedly
Enough of those nights in Metuchen and Metro Park
When you told me you couldn't get enough
Couldn't get enough couldn't get enough of me

The ram steers clear of the rambles
Cleo the hooded asp
The straw disavows the camel
At which it seemed to grasp
The gossip columns link your name
To that loser Antony
Who claims that he's to blame
For your having had enough
Having had enough having had enough of me

TOUCH AND GO

In Brighton beach
The dragon's teeth
Have turned into cold warriors
The situation's thorny
Now Rebecca de Mornay
Was written by Daphne du Maurier
It seems like a first wife
Can really mess up your life
Who knows what may happen
If we don't reap what we sow?
The ideas we haven't planted
May exacerbate our woes
It's touch and go touch and go
It's sometimes touch and go
Touch and go touch and go
It's sometimes touch and go

In Cobble Hill
A catalogue of ills
From which to recuperate

Rather than healing
Our wounded feelings
Have started to suppurate
It seems like pleasure and pain
Are really linked in the brain
Who knows what may happen
After dinner and a show?
We undervalue passion
Until we're in its throes
It's touch and go touch and go
It's often touch and go
Touch and go touch and go
It's often touch and go

Back into a world of wheels within wheels
And a great god coming down hard
Like a hammer coming down on steel
In the Brooklyn Navy Yard

[instrumental]

In Fort Greene
We hope running to seed

Might be a mark of maturity
A strong portcullis
Has been known to lull us
Into a false sense of security
It seems like the Montagues
Are on a really short fuse
Who knows what may happen
When we let resentments grow?
There's a mine under our castle
As to when it's gonna blow
It's touch and go touch and go
It's always touch and go
Touch and go touch and go
It's always touch and go

DOWN WITH THAT

You take the bed
I'll take the chaise
You take the arrowheads
I the polonaise
You take the Raleigh
With the dodgy derailleur
You take Macaulay
I'll take Mailer
You the poisoned pup
I the fat cat
We're breaking up
And I'm down with that
Down with that
I'm really down with that
We're breaking up
And I'm down with that

You take the twin keel
I'll take the gig
You the Oldsmobile

I the Mission fig
You take the condo
And the Real Slim Shady
I Jean-Paul Belmondo
And the '85 Mercedes
As well as the Krups
From Alexanderplatz
Because we're breaking up
And I'm down with that
Down with that
I'm really down with that
We're breaking up
And I'm down with that

Down with the ruling classes
Down with the social elite
They control the masses
They crush us under their feet
That's why we're taking to the streets
That's why we're taking to the streets

[bass and drum instrumental]

You take the Troggs
I'll take the Kinks
You the travelogues
I the tiddlywinks
You take the coasters
and the Tyrone crystal
You take the toaster
I'll take the pistol
You the loving cup
I the fermentation vat
We're breaking up
And I'm down with that
Down with that
I'm really down with that
We're breaking up
And I'm down with that

GOT IT MADE

I've lain here since mid-October
A glade scented with Glade
Just as I've got clean and sober
Just as I've got it made
And just as I'm going under
I've watched my life replayed
It's so downbeat it's a wonder
I ever got it made

Only in woodshop and Spanish
I got a passing grade
That year my father would vanish
He must have got it made
I joined with Jean-Michel Cabot
In the cabinet trade
The tongue and groove of a rabbet
That's how we got it made

That's me in the ruffled collar
The sharp suit and the shades
I look like a million dollars
Look like I've got it made

My heart was suddenly aching
Jess was a nurse's aide
Our child was long in the making
Somehow we got it made
We moved out of that hog-wallow
At Railroad and Kincaid
Though the rent was hard to swallow
We always got it made
The asbestos-lined two-roomer
Plywood sprayed and resprayed
It all adds up to a tumor
And that's how it got made
The doctor was so soft-spoken
He'd split with Medicaid
It looked like something had broken
Just as I'd got it made
The coffin-maker's plug-ugly
There's beauty in his blade
The coffin-lid fits so snugly
Looks like he's got it made

I NEVER KNEW THAT ABOUT YOU

I always knew you were a flirt
For whom men were playthings
There was that time you lost your shirt
In Saratoga Springs
And I don't mean figuratively
I always knew you'd hit pay dirt
When you moved to LA
I knew you'd been willing to convert
From Judaism to the Way
Of Eight Lanes Free
I knew you'd been given enough velvet rope
To hang yourself in CinemaScope
But I never knew that you were untrue
I never knew no I never knew
I never knew that about you

I always knew you were a nag
I heard that first from Tim
You used me as a punching bag
Then went down to the gym

Where Dylan's been known to work it off
I always knew you liked to brag
That your poems smelled of the lamp
I knew you'd flown a Confederate flag
Over your bunk in camp
Mazeltov
I knew you'd always stuck to your guns
After the other side had won
But I never knew you were untrue
I never knew no I never knew
I never knew that about you

Till last night when Tim let slip
You and he had gone lip to lip
Maybe even toe to toe
I never knew I wasn't in the know

[instrumental]

I always knew you were a tease
Half-glimpsed through a half-door
None of the men you brought to their knees
Had a magnitude of more than 4

On your Richter scale
I always knew you were shooting the breeze
About Dylan being a southpaw
I knew experts in tropical disease
Have confused syphilis and yaws
At least once since Captain Cook set sail
I knew you claimed to have met Boom Boom
After some show in the Viper Room
But I never knew you were untrue
I never knew no I never knew
I never knew that about you

CUTTLEBONE

[instrumental]

Here's to the bitter leaf
On top of the flagpole
Here's to what comes to grief
On a coral shoal
You'll be the last overkill
By the First Airborne
You'll be the cornmill
I'll be the corn

Check out the nuclear theater
Where I set the stage
When a private investigator
Asked about your age

You'll be my sole survivor
I'll be your fallout zone
You'll be my pearldiver
I'll be your diving stone

You'll be my pearldiver
I'll be your diving stone

Here's to brisket of beef
Mustard and mayonnaise
Here's to our commander in chief
Out to lunch in the maze
You'll be three bags full
I'll be Samson shorn
You'll be Sitting Bull
At the Little Bighorn

Check out the high pressure
I found so hard to gauge
When you took that refresher
Course on riot and rampage

You'll be my crazy diamond
I'll be your Sierra Leone
You'll be my crime and
I'll be your sentence postponed

Till we've all been sold up the river to Sing Sing
With nothing to show but our clipped wings
And the Pink Floyd album we thought we'd outgrown
But listen to now on one set of earphones

[instrumental]

Here's to the cherished belief
We must sacrifice our kids
Here's to the data thief
Now living off the grid
You'll be a tinker's dam
I'll be your firstborn
You'll be the luckless ram
Caught up in the thorn

Check out the Bay State Hymnal
And my earmarked page
When that cyber criminal
First hacked into your cage

You'll be my Syd Barrett
I'll be your anticyclone
You'll be my red-billed parrot
I'll be your cuttlebone
You'll be my red-billed parrot
I'll be your cuttlebone

[instrumental]

EYEWEAR'S TITLES INCLUDE

EYEWEAR
POETRY

ELSPETH SMITH DANGEROUS CAKES
CALEB KLACES BOTTLED AIR
GEORGE ELLIOTT CLARKE ILLICIT SONNETS
HANS VAN DE WAARSENBURG THE PAST IS NEVER DEAD
BARBARA MARSH TO THE BONEYARD
DON SHARE UNION
SHEILA HILLIER HOTEL MOONMILK
MARION MCCREADY TREE LANGUAGE
SJ FOWLER THE ROTTWEILER'S GUIDE TO THE DOG OWNER
AGNIESZKA STUDZINSKA WHAT THINGS ARE
JEMMA BORG THE ILLUMINATED WORLD
KEIRAN GODDARD FOR THE CHORUS
COLETTE SENSIER SKINLESS
ANDREW SHIELDS THOMAS HARDY LISTENS TO LOUIS ARMSTRONG
JAN OWEN THE OFFHAND ANGEL
A.K. BLAKEMORE HUMBERT SUMMER
SEAN SINGER HONEY & SMOKE
HESTER KNIBBE HUNGERPOTS
MEL PRYOR SMALL NUCLEAR FAMILY
ELSPETH SMITH KEEPING BUSY
TONY CHAN FOUR POINTS FOURTEEN LINES
MARIA APICHELLA PSALMODY
TERESE SVOBODA PROFESSOR HARRIMAN'S STEAM AIR-SHIP
ALICE ANDERSON THE WATERMARK
BEN PARKER THE AMAZING LOST MAN
MANDY KAHN MATH, HEAVEN, TIME
ISABEL ROGERS DON'T ASK
REBECCA GAYLE HOWELL AMERICAN PURGATORY
MARION MCCREADY MADAME ECOSSE
MARIELA GRIFFOR DECLASSIFIED
MARK YAKICH THE DANGEROUS BOOK OF POETRY FOR PLANES
HASSAN MELEHY A MODEST APOCALYPSE
KATE NOAKES PARIS, STAGE LEFT
JASON LEE BURNING BOX
U.S. DHUGA THE SIGHT OF A GOOSE GOING BAREFOOT
DICK WITTS THE PASSAGE: POST-PUNK POETS